The Secret Life of Owls

by J. T. Contardo

Book 2

illustrated by Julie Bryant

Book 2

www.TheSecretLifeSeries.com

mailto: jt@thesecretlifeseries.com

Illustrations and book design by Julie Bryant

www.sweetartdesign.com

Cape Elizabeth, Maine

2012

Dedication

To Dreaming . . . To Aspiring . . . To Knowing . . . To Love . . .

To A New Consciousness for Mankind in 2012 . . .

Through my open window late last night, across the hay, just out of sight,
Strange sounds came from the barn, causing me a fright!

Owls are up while we sleep and tonight's moon-beams reveal,
There's not just one barn owl, but a papa *and* a mama, wanting a meal.

There are so many types of owls, over two hundred, at last count.
You'd need ten fingers on twenty people to count that amount!

Living in every continent on Earth, except Santa's North Pole.
Not even the Elf owl lives there, cause they prefer a warm hole.

Their BIG eyes let them see perfectly, even on the darkest of nights.
One hundred times better than people, and that's without flashlights!

They're tricky too, cause at times they're awake when the sun's out.
But catching rays or hanging at poolside, is not what it's all about.

Most owls hang out alone, stare a lot and tend to look serious.
All have sharp beaks and claws, and are very mysterious.

When their babies arrive, they'll keep them safe and well fed.
The mama protects them, while papa feeds them in bed.

Author, J.T. Contardo

About the Author

J. T. Contardo lives in Maine where he's writing more books for this series, poetry and a memoir depicting his life growing up on the streets of the North Shore of Boston. Recently retired after thirty-five years in the technology sector, he's now embarking on a journey of artistic expression, spiritual awareness, and giving back wherever he can.

When his two sons begged him to stop reading the same picture books over and over, he began writing. His sons then created a list of topics, which has become *The Secret Life Series*. This whimsical story about owls is Book 2. Look for Book 3 *"The Secret Life of Friends!"* and many more topics, available in the coming months.

Email: jt@thesecretlifeseries.com

www.TheSecretLifeSeries.com

www.jtcontardo.blog.com

Look for TheSecretLifeSeries on Facebook and Twitter

Illustrator, Julie Bryant

About the Illustrator

Julie Bryant lives in Napa, California where she was born and raised . . . . . a Napkin!

The illustrations were created using digital watercolors and pencil on a digital drawing tablet.

To contact Julie Bryant, go to sweetartdesign.com for her original books, samples of her book designs, and to view her sweet illustrations.

sweetartdesign.com

And Finally . . .

While walking on Mackworth Island, just north of Portland, Maine in November of 2011, I saw these large birds zooming around over an open field. Upon closer observation, I realized they were Barn owls hunting during the day, which led to this book.

I hope you enjoy the entire series because I sure do enjoy writing them. With the help of talented and beautiful, Julie Bryant, there is no limit to the number of fun and educational topics still to come.

Look for them at *TheSecretLifeSeries.com*, at your local bookstore, online bookseller or a library near you!